Armed with love, fa

Author Evie Moses has written a wonderful book encouraging parents to consciously raise morally sound, respectable children. *Act Like A Parent, Think Like A Child* delivers a no-nonsense approach to "one of the most challenging assignments in the world, the shaping and raising of a human being." Parents are guided through the various stages of childhood with numerous examples of the many pitfalls of parenting and how to avoid them, while providing strength and consistency for the many challenges you face.

Act Like a Parent, Think Like a Child is for everyone – and anyone – who plays a part in raising a child. Parents, grandparents, aunts, uncles, teachers, neighbors, and friends alike will benefit from reading this book.

Terri Coverdale
Community Resource Coordinator
Long Island Community Hospital

***

To put pen to paper is not necessarily difficult, but to imbue one's writing with a depth of understanding and wisdom is not common, nor by happenstance, but by the grace of God. This awesome God tells us that if we lack wisdom, we can ask Him, and He will give generously without finding fault. His brother, James, also tells us that wisdom that is from heaven is, first of all pure, then peace-loving, considerate, submissive, full of mercy and good fruit, impartial, and sincere.

So, to write words of wisdom and sage advice to parents and would-be parents (which this book definitely does) takes an old soul, a willing and listening heart, and the knowledge born by the fire of experience, trial and error, love and commitment, dedication, and awe – not only to the author's children, but to the God who gives freely of His wisdom, love, and grace.

E. Magalene McClarrin

***

Act Like a Parent, Think Like a Child is an imperative necessity and must-have directive for all parents, divulging key essentials for childrearing, especially for the NOW millennial generation and future ones to follow.

In a society that is morally and ethically bewildering for most youth and young adults, this literary work serves as a compass for all parents, extensions of the family, and the village that plays a part in rearing a child. This book not only answers the pondering doubts, or inquiries that each parent or couple struggles with to raise their child, but also serves as a motivation to re-evaluate and alter parental practices to instill character and principles for the next generation to thrive.

If you truly care about the investments that you put into your child's life, then it would be a disservice not to purchase this book!

Tiffany A. Nicholas

***

Firstly, I want to thank you for this awesome book that is filled with valuable information concerning parenting, self-actualization, and responsibilities that come with the "gift" of parenting. Anyone who reads this can find themselves in one scenario or another listed in the chapters. As parenting seems to be phased out in this new day, *Act Like a Parent, Think Like a Child* opens up awareness to parenting issues, needed advice, and guidance on how to take back your role as a parent. I implore all to read this book — even if your children are adults. It can assist you with grandchildren as well.

Dr. Tia Knight-Forbes DNP, FNP-BC

***

Act Like a Parent, Think Like a Child is a great guide to assist parents with breaking dysfunctional habits that are passed down through generations. You can identify your parenting style in the different scenarios described in the book to help you support your good habits and show you the errors of your ways with the not-so-good habits. The end goal is to create loving, well-mannered, productive, and confident children.

Daphne M. Gordon, Ph.D.

Act Like *a* Parent

THINK LIKE A CHILD

EVIE MOSES

Act Like a Parent, Think Like a Child

Book Marketing | Website Design
TimeToGoVirtual.com, LLC
www.genniaholder.com

Book Creation & Design
DHBonner Virtual Solutions, LLC
www.dhbonner.net

ISBN for Paperback: 978-1-7348957-0-4
ISBN for eBook: 978-1-7348957-1-1

Printed in The United States of America

Act Like a Parent

THINK LIKE A CHILD

I dedicate this book to my father and mother who were my introduction to the God I love. Being full of wisdom, they were the beginnings of my set foundation. They were two for the price of one that did not compromise in the values they instilled in us. And, to all of the parents trying their best to parent:

I love and respect you for that.

No one grows up
in a perfect household.
Everyone has a story,
Untold they withhold

Don't be afraid to face
your imperfections.
God gives corrective wisdom
Through prayer and revelation.

Contents

Acknowledgments

I'm giving a shout-out to our neighbors on Inwood Street, South Ozone Park, New York, who cared and looked out for each other's well-being, contributing to a safe environment to both play *and* grow up in. Those who attended Chapel Church of Christ, which was derived from the basement where all of the good teachings were sown. The late Betty Freeman showed my sisters, my brother, and me the love and affection that was vitally needed at the time. Esther Wilcox was our escape in Far Rockaway when we needed an outlet. John Singer showed us and took us to places we had never been to broaden us Queens kids' horizons. To Terence, Lindora, and Darlene, *love always*. To my husband, Tim, you understood and knew my worth. Lastly, Tajee and Tyra, you guys are my inspiration. I'm better because of you. Thank you, Jesus!

Introduction

"Do you know what you're having?"
"Yes, I'm actually having a boy, and you?" I'm finally having a girl after the fifth try. My husband is so excited that he's finally getting the little princess he's always wanted…"

When I was nineteen years old, I had complications driving, not realizing it was my vision. It was not until it worsened that I went to an eyeglass store. When my vision was checked, they told me that the issue I had was too complicated for them and that I would need to see a specialist. Tears came to my eyes when the doctor told me that I was going blind, caused by a disease called keratoconus, and there was no cure. By the time I am pronounced legally blind, I would then be eligible for a corneal transplant.

By the time I was ready for my first eye surgery, I had two children; one was under two-years-old, and the other was three. They were playing in the living room when I came home from the hospital with a large plastic cup bandaged over my eye. As young as they were, they sensed that I was not well and knew not to abruptly hug me, as was the norm. Instead, they both watched and waited until I sat down before gingerly hugging me.

I felt an overwhelming rain of empathy and compassion from them. The love that I had displayed to them was the same love they were now returning to me. Although they didn't know the doctor gave me strict orders to — under no circumstances — lift anything heavy and to keep the eye guarded, so that the graph would heal effectively, they proceeded to play at a bit of a distance, with consideration.

The Bible talks of training up a child in the way they should go (Proverbs 22:6). It was because of their balanced training prior to my surgery that their instincts, as well as a sense of compassion, played a significant role in my peace of mind. I loved it. I could heal while still being able to cautiously interact with my children.

However, I was intentional about training them while using discipline, love, and balance. That was something I desperately wanted for this woman (I'll call her Maggie) as we chatted one afternoon:

> Her little boy said, "Mom, let's play." He was an only child, about five-years-old, so she felt the need to accommodate him. Once they were wrestling and laughing, however, things took a turn. The anger in her son overtook him as he told his mom, with clenched fists, "I want to be in control." She talked about how she had to calm him down and chuckled while explaining to me that it wasn't the first and only occurrence.

Sometime later, as 'Maggie' and her son were with me in public, she told him three times to have a seat next to her, but he refused. Embarrassed by the stares of others, she pleaded with him, and when that didn't work, she made a proposal — he wouldn't be going to McDonald's unless he listened.

That day, it wasn't working. So, as she held his arm, she gave him a lecture on the importance of listening. It still didn't work. After watching this for a while, I told her, "He knows you don't mean it."

She asked me, "What do you mean? Of course, he knows I mean it!" I said, "Without volume, change the tone of your voice, slow your words down, and look him in the eye... mean what you say."

She did it, and it worked.

Then, she shared with me that she had been having problems with him and that her husband worked odd hours, so he was not involved as needed.

I reminded her of how her child becomes aggressive when she plays with him, informing her that this was his way of seeking attention, while marking his territory to gain full control of her. I recommended that she create boundaries – say what you mean and mean what you say, and no more physical games that should be with his peers. The time she shared with her child shouldn't include *who will conquer who*; you would have already lost the child's respect. There are games you can play that won't allow him authority and are fun.

. . . .

Love with boundaries.

. . . .

We talked from time to time. Sharing wisdom from a place of love and concern, I walked her through it. She applied the advice given, and although the father was present but not engaging, mom didn't allow that to keep her from doing her part. It was sometimes tiresome, picking up the slack for his dad, but she stayed the course because she knew their son's future as a man depended on it.

Every now and then, she and her son would bump heads, but it would never cross the boundaries that were set, and she would often say, "You know, I'm really enjoying my son, and his dad is missing out." She was amazed by how far he had come in character and behavior. Although he's closer to his mom, he respects and loves both parents because of her balance of love and discipline. Without belittling her husband, she was able to build a foundation for her son that counteracted the father's inability to connect because no one had connected with him when he was a child.

Just because a household has issues doesn't mean things can't be worked on through wisdom, communication, and understanding; sanding and smoothing edges develop a good character out of a not-so-good situation.

'Maggie' is now the proud momma of a young man who graduated top of his class with the world as his oyster. He also does not have to repeat the mistakes his father made with him because he learned unconditional love, with the boundaries set by a loving mom while having respect for both of his parents. Best of all, the bond between mother and son has healthy boundaries, with love and respect on both sides. It is a beautiful thing to witness.

Many of us are engrossed in our financial security. We know that the sooner we start investing in our retirement, the greater our return later. All of our ducks are perfectly aligned, and any loss or uncertainty in our investments sends people into a grave depression. It is highly important to invest wisely and hope for the best. Regarding our children, early investment is momentous. How the world functions is based on who is running it. Our children today are tomorrow's "who." The most significant investment in life is the raising, guidance, and leading of a child — planning for a better world and a better future.

As parents, we need different perspectives, to learn from others so that we avoid mistakes, and raise children that we not only love, but whom we like. We are the people, with a nurturing eye, that hold the children up to specific standards. We keep them accountable so they can be well *and do well* in life.

The responsibility of raising people who will be kind, considerate, loving, humble, and responsible is a considerable weight for us as parents. To believe that there are perfect families with perfect children, you would be insinuating that there are perfect people. There are no perfect people, which is why there are no perfect families or children. Wisdom sets a foundational guide to ironing out our imperfections.

What if, at one point, you felt that you had it all together as a parent, only to question yourself as to where you went wrong? Why don't siblings love and care for each other? How do I not raise a bully? How do I raise a child that is not subjected to being bullied?

> "It takes a village to raise a child."
> —African Proverb

Being all that your child can be starts with good character. Without good character, there is no integrity; without integrity, there is no honor; without honor, there is no respect.

The old above ground pool in our backyard that was once a play, eat, and rest stop for children, was the hot spot in the neighborhood. This played an important role in my watching the development of children. Children were drawn to our home because there was fun and food. Whenever the weekend came, or school was out, we were always open for business with open arms. I had the opportunity to pour into those children, along with my own. You would be amazed to know that, when you have positive people around you that love and care for your children the way you do, it increases your effectiveness in raising your children. It's called 'a village.'

Allow me to be a part of your 'village.' And I invite you to be a part of mine. We all live in a society where we are impacted by someone's child every day. From the toddler you see in the stroller to the adult who is your co-worker, someone has had a hand in raising them.

We are the people with a nurturing eye that holds the children up to certain standards. We keep them accountable to be well, and to do well, in life.

With the information I will share in the pages that follow, I hope to have a part in supporting you as you build a foundation, breaking negative cycles and circumstances that offset God's plans for you and your children's lives.

1

What Baggage
Are You Bringing?

Before we dig into the details, let's first take a look at ourselves . . .living with others, having close ties, whether in marriage or having children, presents "mirrored moments." It is having to face yourself through someone else's eyes and being accountable.

I thought I was a decent Christian — no drama, chose my circle wisely, tried to do what's right. I thought I was as good as I'd ever been and was ever going to get – until I got married. I brought in baggage I had no idea I had, swearing that it was not me because I thought I was just "fine." My definition of *fine* was the baggage I didn't know I was carrying. It was my marriage and my children that God used to refine my *fine*. I submitted to His wisdom, and He showed me myself through love, discipline, and balance in those "mirrored moments."

You must be willing to face the truths in yourself before you can help yourself or anyone else. I realized early on that I was not perfect, nor will I ever be; there's always improvement to be made within our thought process and actions. Thankfully, the wisdom of God is perfect. So, be open to self-assessment, heart cleansing, and soul-searching, in order to be receptive to His wisdom.

Bringing baggage into a relationship — your experiences and upbringing — affects how you speak to, set boundaries, and discipline your child. It takes courage to be honest about the baggage you carry, but to be the parents, our children's lives depend on it. You've got to remove the blinders to see what, and if, you're projecting onto your children.

As we mature, we should care more about personal growth to become a better human being. Becoming a better spouse or parent involves changing our behavior. Let's look at ways that our past experiences can negatively affect the way we raise our children.

WERE YOU A DEPRIVED CHILD?

You say you grew up poorly. Your parent, or parents, didn't have much to give you. You had to wear hand-me-downs. Your family made use of government assistance programs. You felt like you were an outcast. You were made fun of, or even bullied because you didn't have the latest or trendiest clothing to wear. Your parents couldn't afford extra activities; such as sports, dance, movies, vacations and so on. You watched other children and thought, *I wish.*

Now, you're an adult that's coveting for your children. Your children will never want or long for anything. From their toddler stages, they cry for not a need, but for every want, and you anxiously make it happen. They then begin to master "demand and supply" . . . they demand, you supply. Love only consists of what you can give or do for them. Before they can utter or request, you've already pulled the rabbit out of your hat, whether affordable or not, jumping through hoops and climbing towers like "Mission impossible."

Some "missions" need to be impossible. Johnny or Jane must learn to hear phrases like "NO," "not now," "not at this time," "I can't afford that," "You'll have to wait," "Let's see how well you do in..." These terms are incredibly vital. It will save them from the attitude of entitlement that the world and everyone in it revolve around them. Later, when faced with disappointments, they can't cope. These terms will cause them to be resilient to life's rejections. They will proceed through life with caution and fewer wounds.

....

Some missions need to be impossible.

....

You must teach them the importance of contentment, gratitude, and appreciation in and of life. So, stop being the "cash cow," "all-season Santa," running birthday specials all year. There's absolutely nothing wrong with pampering your children, especially when they're well-behaved, not spoiling them rotten to the core. Without balance, your child will begin to overwhelm you. Slow your roll and think it through before you play the "super parent that can." Just because you can, doesn't mean you should. Keep it balanced. They will respect and appreciate you more for it. If not now, then later.

IS THIS YOUR "MIRACLE" CHILD?

You had difficulty bearing a child, and it finally happened. You now have what you've desperately longed for. Your child says, "I will easily be running this show."

Yes, your child must be a priority, however, not to the extent of holding your entire life hostage, living in a prison camp with your child as the overseer with the keys in hand. You can't make any sudden moves unless they permit you to. The life you once knew is no more. You've lost your identity to Johnny. Johnny is raising you to be what he wants you to be. You signed on as a parent to be trained by your child. If you don't get a handle on this, it will be difficult for not just you, but others as well.

For example, you suddenly need a babysitter after staying home for five years. Your husband was laid off, and you must return to work to stay afloat. Johnny is cared for, but not idolized by the babysitter. This is not working out well for Johnny. Johnny doesn't care that there are other children to tend to, so he throws a never-ending tantrum, and the babysitter says, "Sorry, but I can no longer keep your Johnny."

Understand that Johnny's behavior outside of your home depends on the training inside of the home. The balanced foundation of love and discipline you set for your child allows them to function well with others, with or without you. You were born before Johnny, so act like you know more than Johnny. Johnny can't have control if it belongs to you. You must have the upper hand, maintaining structure and stability. Do not lose yourself in your child; otherwise, your child will never find you or even care to know you.

CONTROLLED OR CONTROLLING?

Passive versus aggressive. You're of a passive nature. Maybe you were brought up in a passive, laid back, easy-going home, so that's all you know. Please recognize early when your Johnny Junior didn't take after you and your people.

Own this fact sooner than later or else... Remember, they share DNA with you, along with another. Don't sit and make excuses for Johnny. Handle Johnny. Be honest and deal with the fact that Johnny didn't take after you. Johnny is aggressive and strong-willed. You then have to alter your personality, customizing yourself to the needs of Johnny. Turn up the heat so that Johnny sees whose will is stronger.

The child will test you by touching something you specifically told him not to. You say, "Don't touch it" in a commanding voice. If you mean what you say, it will be convincing; however, if you don't really mean it, the child will ignore you. If it's said with a convincing and authoritative tone, you may not even need to raise your voice. A child can look into your eyes with radar to detect strength or weakness. Mean what you say and say what you mean consistently. If you catch it early, it's a smoother road ahead, minimizing your stress level.

....

Don't be controlling; be in control.

....

On the other hand, if you are of an aggressive nature and your child is found to be passive, you will need to turn down the heat a few notches, depending on the child. The reason why I say depending on the child is because some children can be manipulative, while portraying sweet and passive antics. You must be watchful and in tune with that particular child. There is no one size for all. Every parent must have a sign that says, "I'm not to be fooled with."

When you're controlling, you throw orders and threats around, and it's noneffective. The child will not respond to or take empty words seriously, not even if you yell them. The first time you speak, the child should listen without you having to repeat yourself over and over again. Mean it the first time you say it.

Whether you are too passive or too aggressive, some children easily listen, and some children can be defiant. Adjust yourself to the needs of a child if you find that you're moving close to either extreme.

LIVING VICARIOUSLY THROUGH YOUR CHILD

You want your child to become all that you were or weren't. You had low self-esteem. You didn't fit in or fought to fit in. You were never the best at anything. You weren't the greatest singer, dancer, musician... You weren't the captain of the football team or the cheerleading team. You didn't win First Place in the Spelling Bee contest. You felt like the runt of the litter.

You weren't Mr. or Mrs. popular. You wanted to be noticed, and you weren't. Or, you've experienced having all of this and need someone in your life to continue your legacy. You are now a parent raising your child to be all they could be in your army of "Yes, you can"!

You stop beating yourself up for not fulfilling your own expectations and are now beating your child up to fulfill those expectations. They are held accountable for what you missed out on, or what you didn't complete. You're pushing them hard to fit in and be the best. "Let's go! I'm signing my Jane up for dance lessons, and at the time of the recital, my Jane must be front and center." "Hey coach, why is my Johnny on the bench?" "We don't have time to live in the moment." "Chop chop! Let's go."

While you're fighting and pushing to win by your standards, your child is living under the pressure of your shadow, either miserable or thinking that life and relationships are based on being the best and winning at all costs. The young soldier needs to learn how to gracefully stand down sometimes and be okay.

Note: Tossing children around to every sport and activity cannot compensate for quality time being spent with them. Yes, be their number one supporter, but careful of your intent behind it. Be sure to understand what's going on inside of your child before you conjure up all of the insecurities in them that you fought to escape within yourself.

THE FIGHT TO STAY YOUNG

Growing older can be challenging for some parents. My advice is don't grow shamefully, but grow gracefully. You were distraught when you graduated high school/college. You knew that this was a sign of getting older. You dealt with it, getting on with your life, yet your heart remains in your past. You're underdeveloped, trying to function as an adult.

The "school days" just won't leave you alone. So, you give your underage child a pass in doing things that he or she is not ready for, or maybe shouldn't be doing at all for cool points. So that you could fit in, as the parent, you didn't put reins on them, so if you can't beat them, you join them. Your child accepted you, and now you feel young at heart. This is not looking good for you, the parent. Looking for acceptance from your children?

You can develop a buddy system with your child with boundaries and balance. You had your day; now it's theirs. Don't allow your insecurities to leave room for them to dishonor you. As time moves on, you can still enjoy life in parent mode. Allow your child to respect your eldership and your wisdom. Maintain boundaries so that the line of respect always stands. When that child gets older, requesting your advice or guidance will honor and respect you enough.

It's beautiful to hang out with your children, but you don't have to revert in time to do so; you will still have a good time. If you fight age, your child will fight age as if it's a disease. It should be thought of as a blessing and something to look forward to with no shame or excuses. They will learn how to embrace every stage of life if you do it first. If we live in the past, we will never embrace the present moments of our lives.

I encourage the bond of parents and children; however, I always remember the words "respect" and "honor," which are what many youths lack in our society today. An employee will respond to the supervisor according to how the supervisor carries himself/ herself.

···
Let your age be respected, not disregarded.
···

Never let it be said — or even thought — that you hold a tinge of jealousy for your child. Choose to be happy and content in every stage of your life. Live and let live.

YOU'RE NOT THE BEST EXAMPLE OF A PARENT

When you find that you're not good at parenting, search yourself, and discover what it is about you that needs to change so that you can be a better example for the sake of your child. You can't teach what you've never been taught. If you defend your child when they are wrong, you've been played for a fool.

If your child is present while you do this, that's worse than the crime itself. The harbor is worse than the thief. So, don't go screaming and yelling at the teacher if you know your child is dead wrong. Put an end to it. Later, if not corrected, your child will never respect you, the teacher, the classmate, the coworker, the supervisor, the police officer, and even their spouse.

The little monster you created becomes the adult monster in society. Don't be embarrassed now; learn and do better, or you will be embarrassed later. There is no harm in asking a Veteran Parent (VP) for advice. VP's are those that have raised their children to be honorable and productive citizens through perfections and imperfections, with wisdom to offer. The problem is that some parents don't want to hear the truth about their parenting flaws.

Remember, it's for the good of the child, as well as yourself, unfolding the mounds of pressure on your shoulders. It's not easy; it's work. But if anyone is worth the work, it's your child. Pay now or pay later. When you lack understanding, it's ok to lend an ear to a trusted source for further thought. Don't let your pride destroy what can be corrected early.

It takes a safe 'village' to assist with children. If you must change the people you hang with (including family), then do so to save your child. Watch for, link up with, and learn from the people who have integrity.

....
Learn better; do better.
....

Don't ever think you can do your dirt behind your child's back, thinking that they won't learn of it. Children have a keen sense of smell for fraudulence. When they see integrity, they will display integrity; however, if they sense the opposite, they can display that, too.

This may not be easy to admit or even see yourself, but we all bring past experiences, shortcomings, and hurts with us. It's baggage, and whether we're aware of it or not, if left unaddressed, they factor into how we discipline, love, and set boundaries with our children. Here are some:

- You lacked the experience of having a mother or father.
- You are so in love with the fact that you get to offer what you never received.
- You're a single parent trying to overcompensate for the lack of two parents.
- You find it difficult to say "no" while trying to gain their love.
- You're separately housed and co-parenting.
- One or both parents are competing to see who can look like "the good guy."
- You're in a dysfunctional marriage or relationship, and when contending with the dysfunction, the child is overlooked.
- You didn't have much growing up, so you feel your child must have everything, whether affordable or not.
- You had difficulty conceiving or carrying, and it finally happened, so you idolize the child.
- You're of a passive nature, and your child is naturally aggressive -- or vice versa -- so their will supersedes your will (they're training you to be what they want you to be).

- You want them to become all that you never were, so you are living vicariously through them.
- You battle with insecurity, fighting to remain young, so your child becomes your bestie (of equal rank).
- You're not the best example as a parent because we can't teach what we don't live.

The category you fall into — or next to — will bring truth to the forefront. Your truth belongs to you, and no one else. However, you also own the responsibility to clear vision, release for change, and transform. It hits a nerve or two at first; yet, when the truth is faced, let freedom ring and let peace reign.

Our society wastes time watching and keeping up with others. It's all about imaging a mirage to one another, while pushing and promoting oneself as a product, not a person. What one presents themselves as doesn't always line up with what's inward. Take the time to understand and know the brand of luggage you hold. You deserve the timeout to do so. Your truth is the essence of you. You'll never need an audience.

Befriend it!

Understanding that your child (or children) is a combination of yourself and the other parent, first determine whether you and the other parent are passive or aggressive personalities, then assess your child's demeanor. If your demeanor and your child's differ, what skill/strategy will you employ to effectively parent without breaking that child's spirit?

If you have more than one child and their personalities vary greatly, can you parent them the same way? Why or why not?

_____

_____

_____

_____

_____

_____

_____

_____

_____

_____

WHAT BAGGAGE ARE YOU BRINGING?

2

There Is No Such Thing As Perfection

Time is of the essence. So, don't waste time trying to be the perfect parent. Focus on being a wise parent. Perfection is not in the equation, merely because a child needs room for errors, just as we did to develop in a healthy manner.

There's no perfect life,
but there is perfect peace.

Facing imperfections helps one to learn from errors with a sense of humility, which leads to integrity. The most challenging assignment in the world is the shaping and raising of another human being. Remember, you only get one shot, so you must make wise decisions.

There are no hard and fast rules for raising a child. But when you're a first-time parent, you read books, follow the gurus, and you get loads of advice from well-meaning people, wanted or not. You might also compare yourself to what other mothers are doing, not knowing what's happening behind the scenes in their life. How do you decipher what's best for you?

THE EARLY YEARS

At about six months, your baby's personality starts to manifest. They move from feeling you to now watching you. Little Johnny or Jane is learning cause and effect. If I do this, what will happen?

For example, if I scream with fury after deliberately dropping my toy on the ground five times, they will panic, feeling sorry for me and keep passing it back to me because I am building my foundation. How you react matters. Put the toy away and address their attention elsewhere in a calm, authoritative manner.

By the time they're a year old, they are walking or about to. They've gained independence while marking their territory. Let's see what I can get into and get away with. On top of that, they've mastered the word "NO" by now and are making their own decisions. Your dominance is challenged to test if you're really in charge.

These are the small things that, if not addressed, become a huge problem later. So, when you say the word "NO," you must look that adorable rascal in the eyes and mean it with authority. They have exceptional instincts to determine whether or not your "NO" holds more weight than their "no."

When they've come to the understanding of who's in charge, the terrible twos won't be so terrible. You now have time to enforce your authority, keeping them safe and sound. Children become more teachable when they are disciplined. And you have more time to love on them, as opposed to yelling and threatening them with empty promises of consequences. Consistency builds trust. Say what you mean and mean what you say, then stick to it. Establishing this between the ages of one and five will lead to a more productive and wholesome upbringing.

Remember, you're not just caring for your child's basic needs; you are molding and building character in them. Despite how society feels, saying let them have their own mind and make their own choices is not wise, because their brains are underdeveloped and are in desperate need of your guidance. They cannot train themselves; it's impossible. If you try it, you will reap what you sow.

YOU ARE THEIR DRIVING FORCE

Now, as they are growing, stop looking at them, focusing on how and what you would like them to be and *gear* them in the direction they need to be. Be quick to make corrections as soon as necessary. Don't be lazy and let it slide. There's the old saying, "give them an inch, and they will take a mile." Get over how cute they are and make sure their character or personality is what it should be.

Maneuver your gears to adjust or adapt to situations to bring satisfactory results within the substance of their personality.

Because no two children are alike, you must understand the type of child you're dealing with. For example, if your child seems like they are challenged by low self-esteem, it is you that must bring them to a balance without breaking their spirit.

If your child has high self-esteem, that might also be a problem that needs to be addressed. They then need to be humbled in order to have a character of balance. Children want to love and respect you as a parent, but it must be taught.

THE ADOLESCENT TO TEEN YEARS

For some children, learning this comes easy if they do not have a stubborn nature, but those that do must be broken. You see, what's broken you can build. Leaving adolescence coming to the teenage years, you would have set a foundation that will establish what is and isn't acceptable.

Now that child is held accountable for whatever choices and decisions they make because they were taught better. When they make life mistakes — and they will — the love and discipline will challenge them to learn, grow, and be better from it.

Commands are in place as the foundation, starting when you realize they comprehend you, which is around ten months of age to four-years-old, with plenty of love and affection. Then choices can be presented to prick their conscience at about six to sixteen-years-old, so that reasoning is reasonable. Of course, ages vary depending on the child's development.

Communication is vital. Stay watchful, always lending an ear to what they have to say because you must know how and what they're thinking. Having an understanding of their thought process will better assist you in their guidance. So, listen very carefully when conversing with them. Ask questions and be patient to listen to the answer, so you can address whatever the topic or issue wisely.

THE SIXTH SENSE

Sometimes as a parent, you know something isn't right. It's a gut feeling. You instinctively know what no book can tell you. It's your sixth sense. A deeper level of perception. It is what helps us gauge the scale of balance. The scale can't tip over on either side; it needs to remain somewhat in the middle. In other words, proportion the complexity of their personalities. Some children internalize their thoughts or find it difficult to express them. They must be monitored attentively. Too far to the left or right can become a downward spiral effect.

As a parent, it is the insight into your child's real personality. Your eyes and ears, combined with your emotions, can sometimes fool or blind you. You can be easily led astray, finding yourself lost because you can't figure out what's going on with your child.

It is almost like being out-of-body, analyzing your child from an unbiased standpoint. It's a deeper level of perception. There's an old saying that says, "you can't see the picture when you're in the frame." The sixth sense allows you to X-ray and scan the child's demeanor. A feeling that, when used starting in the child's early years, you can foresee their road ahead. Then you can put up roadblocks, caution signs, signals, and directions as you're guiding them through this thing called life. As they explore life, you are the navigation system.

Keep communication as your GPS device, with love and discipline hand in hand. Be relatable without compromising what's right or what's best. Sometimes when we as parents have a lot on our plate to deal with, we don't make time to pay attention. Make the time and be observant of what's going on with them and how they react and respond to different situations. If you're not in tune with the direction they are headed, you can't give instruction.

With a "sixth sense," your child will say, "my parents know me so well it's difficult to pull the wool over their eyes." Yes, mistakes made in life are natural; however, what is willfully done after being warned wouldn't be referred to as a mistake, but a choice. Guiding them in the right direction early will assist them in making better choices later.

Also, use discernment to protect your children from predators, which come in all ages, sizes, and disguises. Don't allow them to feel comfortable with any and everybody; be selective with who you allow around your children and stay observant of those around them. Teach them about their bodies and the importance of protecting themselves. Make sure they know that they can speak to you about anything.

....
Discernment is the sixth sense.
....

Remember, however, that there is absolutely no one-size-fits-all. Even identical twins think differently. You can dress them alike, but their character and personality should be attended to as individuals.

We all come into the world with individual brains and mindsets. You can copy, imitate, or follow someone, even share the same interests, but no two minds are identical in thought.

REFLECTION

As your child matures (even as an infant or toddler), why is it important to allow them to make age-appropriate choices? How will you balance the scale between developing the child's ability to make wise choices and dealing with the reward or consequence of their choice?

_____

_____

_____

_____

_____

_____

_____

_____

_____

_____

_____

_____

_____

3

The Parenting
Essentials

Plenty of the problems within our society are based on our childhood trainer. How well one does in their field of work is based on their training. A world champion boxer's success and well-being, no matter how gifted he is, is inspired by his trainer. The trainer has complete access, control, and the responsibility of producing and bringing out the best in that boxer. The fruit of the trainer's labor is evident in how the boxer maneuvers throughout his career, whether defeated or undefeated.

Parents, you are the trainer, and your children are the trainees. I must say that most of the problems that have brushed past my ears are attributed to the fruit of the trainer. I have always made a conscious effort not to discuss my children too much because, when others were complaining about theirs, I wasn't complaining about mine. I felt reluctant for not having gone through a lot of the issues they experienced, and I never wanted to make them feel worse than they already did, so I refrained from discussing my children.

Not being arrogant or judgmental, I was focused on keeping an eye on my children all the more. I'm seeing now that parents relish, promote, and cosign their children's poor behavior. Why should I feel guilty about discussing my children's good behavior? They are not perfect, and I would never hold them to be.

However, what they do have is good character, having been raised with a lot of love, discipline, and balance – what I consider essential for training a child. However, to whatever degree of an issue I was facing, I would share how I dealt with that issue; they would be amazed at my tactics in dealing with both of my children. One thing's for sure, these training stages are to be handled by starting from the beginning years of childhood. In other words, there will be issues that you will face in parenting, but you must meet them head-on and do not, under any circumstances, ignore them.

My children understood my stance on what was acceptable and what was not through discipline, love, and balance. What if your child is misunderstood, labeled, or underestimated due to a lack of these three necessities? They may never reach their full potential in life if that's the case. Therefore, let's discuss these three essentials in more detail.

DISCIPLINE IS ESSENTIAL

The identity of your child is formed and molded by you, the parent. They cannot understand who or what they are without your guidance. Stop letting them choose how they want to be. They cannot build their own character, that's your job.

- Your job is to parent.
- You are accountable for your child's well-being.
- Your responsibility is to raise your child to reach their own highest potential with a healthy balance of love and discipline.

Some of you threatened to or sent your children to the military because you missed the training window. Talk show counselors have their work cut out for them.

Institutions are overpopulated with adults that were once children with great potential. People can't work together professionally due to a lack of respect. Marriages are not even surviving for two years. Teachers are giving up because they're stressed out from the challenges they face with students and their parent's lack of cooperation.

Some of you love your child/children, but they seem to aggravate your last nerve. You love them, but you dislike them because you didn't put your foot down early on.

These are just some of the repercussions. If you take a look at the world around you, you will see that there is a shortage of loyalty attached to family and friendships. This is not to judge; it is to help. Moral conduct has declined over the years.

....

Don't try to be perfect... be wise.

....

There will be times that your decisions do not go along with the majority. You will be saying 'no' when the other parents are saying 'yes.' Once again, it's your instincts, values, and love for your child. Don't abuse it. Own it and utilize it! Think of it this way . . . if you allow the majority to influence your household, you are forfeiting your right as the parent.

LOVE IS ESSENTIAL

An unloved child is an empty child, left exposed and vulnerable to any entity that opposes love. The thing about love is that it's authentic. What's authentic is true, and what's true is pure. It cannot be disguised or mimicked. Love replaces and can fill all gaps in a child's rearing, no matter who or where they come from.

Love presents itself as kind, strong, humble, and patient. Now, just imagine all of this in you and being generated from you to your child. This is how love and discipline go hand in hand. When you love your child, you want to show them the right way, and when they go left, you correct them because love cares and is concerned enough for your child's well-being to do so.

Love allows you to live in your truth and gives you the strength to stand in your truth, correcting and bringing an end to foolishness. Love without discipline is dysfunctional love. The friend you say you love is about to encounter the deadly cliff that's not in their view; you have a clear view of it with no intention of warning them . . . that's not love. Johnny will not embrace, appreciate, and respect your love without correction. What if he's mad at you for the moment? Be strong in your love that ties to his well-being.

Always remember this . . . you can't house love and hate at the same time. It's like trying to lighten a dark room with darkness. The bitterness you, the parent, are holding on to can disrupt your ability to raise a child lovingly. If your tree carries rotten apples, what falls off will be none other than rotten apples. That's why, in looking at your child, you disown the fact that you're looking at yourself in the mirror. Bitterness will never let you see the truth of this. Bitterness will breed only bitterness. Do what you must to dismiss the negative vibe you carry because with or without saying a word, your child feels what you internalize.

....
When your love is authentic,
your discipline will be respected.
....

BALANCE IS ESSENTIAL

We started by talking about raising your children using three parenting essentials: discipline, love, and balance. But what is balance, really? Well, let me give you the factual (dictionary) definition:

"Balance is an even distribution of weight, enabling someone or something to remain upright and steady. It is the stability of one's mind or feelings. To keep or put (something), or in this case, someone in a steady position so that it does not fall."

I was blessed to have two beautiful children. My son was the first, and my daughter was born second. I was challenged by the fact that my son was born with a serious temper. It was as if he knew something that we didn't know. His cry was irregular. It sounded vengeful, loud, and intense. He was a beautiful baby, yet he had not a sensitive bone developing in his little body. I realized that he had a strong will.

At five months, he would crawl and accidentally hit his head hard. He would keep going like nothing happened, never needing to be coddled. He began walking at the age of nine months and dared anyone, other than his parents, to touch or pick him up. If you dared, he would either bite or head-bang you because he didn't want to be bothered. Toys were his love, not people. He would play by himself for hours, needing no attention, only food in a timely manner.

Despite his ways, we still set boundaries. His personality said he was insensitive, but his actions were obedient because he had "learned" early on. With that being established, I was able to love him out of his frustration, giving him all the unwanted affection, periodically, without overwhelming him until he adapted.

Now, on the other side of the coin, my daughter was the complete opposite. It was from one extreme to the other. She was born with the sweetest aura. A gentle soul, she was. If you looked at her wrong or too intensely, she would burst into tears. You can't make this up. She was overly sensitive and very observant. Now, this would work if the rest of society stayed out of her way or she could stay home for the rest of her life, but that's not realistic.

I had to make sure that she felt safe while building her up to be stronger, without breaking her spirit of purity. I had to teach her early that the rest of the world may not subject themselves to her sensitivity. So, we had to create a backbone for her to get along at home with her sibling, as well as when attending school, which carries over into the workforce.

Yes, this is the short story version of it, but the point I'm making is that I had to balance them steadily so that they don't have to keep falling. My son is quite a young man with sensitivity. He still has a tough side, but his discipline keeps it in line. My daughter is still sweet and full of compassion for others, but she's no pushover.

The food you eat should be a healthy balance for the body to function steadily. If you eat or drink too much of anything, it can throw your entire system off. It's the same way with children. Perfection is not an option, so don't kid yourself while trying to achieve it. We take it one day at a time with understanding and wisdom. Train them so that you not only love them, but like them in order to enjoy them.

My children were the total opposite in personality, and yet, they were trained to respect and love each other. If you behave as an authoritative peacemaker, they become peacemakers. When you teach loyalty, they will know loyalty. It's much more effective when applied early, but better late than never.

You can predict what your baby's gender will be, but you can't predict their nature until they arrive. Their nature is guided through you, the parent. Be watchful and observant to guide them. No child is born with an instruction tag that says *let me raise myself to be what I choose to be.* You are their greatest influence. You are entirely responsible for being the best you can be in raising your children. Cherish and teach them the right path to walk, even if the way seems narrow and unpopular. Popularity holds no strength or substance in character; it's a fluke that passes eventually.

Teach them, reach them.

REFLECTION

Take this time to reflect on the three essential keys mentioned (Love, Discipline, Balance). What is your definition, and how do you demonstrate each of these to your child/children? Is there an adequate balance? How will you correct, if needed?

_____

_____

_____

_____

_____

_____

_____

_____

_____

_____

_____

_____

_____

_____

_____

_____

4

Facing Diverse Issues

Thinking of bringing a child into this world? A word to the wise — I'm not one to sugarcoat things, so I want to say it as plain as I can — having children is rewarding and beautiful and amazing. But it's not easy, even when you have support. Raising children is hard work.

Deciding to have a child is a very important decision to make. Unless you choose to be a parent alone, don't consciously bring children into the world without two consenting parties. This way, the child is received as a blessing rather than a burden. Don't do it vindictively, for validation, or any selfish reason that has to do with no consideration for the child.

Thinking of having children? Start thinking of who is in your trusted 'village' and be sure to include (VPs) other mothers. It is essential to learn from the experiences of other moms, as they can be the voice of reason when you're at your wit's end.

Be honest about being ready to give all that it takes to give in parenting. The work to plan a wedding is never more significant than the work to keep the marriage. A wedding is one day, a marriage is the rest of your life. Just as the process of raising a child extends far beyond the process of pregnancy. Pregnancy is nine months; raising a child is at least eighteen years and beyond. Although your relationship changes as they grow, you never stop worrying, caring, and being there for them.

Now, I want to cover the different scenarios we face as parents. The weight of discipline is not always distributed evenly. Whether divorced, separated, widowed, absentee, or unsupportive parent... life happens.

Children have different personalities. Families have different dynamics, so comparing your household to someone else's doesn't work. We must adjust how we discipline and train our children, regardless, based on our unique situation and parent accordingly.

I want to share a few strategies and tactics you can use, depending on your parenting situation, to have healthy boundaries using the parenting essentials of love, discipline, and balance.

TWO-PARENT HOME

I came up with what I call the "Red light, green light system" that worked wonders for my husband and me.

Formula:

● + ● = ●

✓ + ✓ = ✓

● + ✓ = ✓

You're in a stable relationship and raising your child together. You have the hands-on support you need – to whatever degree. Your family dynamics are pretty much together, and it appears that everything is under control. Yet, your child has learned you both. He/she knows which parent will bow and which one will stand. The red light green light system works like this:

Parent 1 says No ● Parent 2 say No ●
No equals No ●

Parent 1 says Yes ✓ Parent 2 says Yes ✓
Yes equals Yes ✓

Parent 1 says No ● Parent 2 says Yes ✓
No equals yes ✓

When the lights do not match, confusion in the child's mind begins, although it is short-lived because they've found a loophole, obtaining the stamp of approval for the takeover. Parents, you've lost control. The child will continue to manipulate the one who says yes and may build resentment for the one that says no. It is important that both parents stay on the same page.

Even at times – if and when – you disagree (it's normal), make an effort to handle it without the child's eyes and ears. If they get wind, they start pulling out tactical weapons, causing division between the two of you; the child will lose honor for both of you, and their training and rearing will be compromised.

As long as both parents have the child's best interest at heart, never let the child build a wedge between the two of you. Children are always watching; if they can manipulate a situation, they surely will. They should never be burdened or pulled into any parental arguments. They are not on your level of authority nor maturity. It may force them to take sides or even rebel. Remember, two red lights or two green lights. That's it.

SINGLE PARENTS

You're on your own raising your child. Your pity party becomes their pity party play. You feel alone and abandoned. For this, you're frustrated because you realize how much work it entails to raise a child. You say negative comments in front of the child about the absentee parent. You're so miserable that all of your energy is driven by this issue. So, your problem becomes your child's problem because you set it up that way.

You're not the first, and definitely not the last, single parent on the earth. So, you feel the need to give and do above and beyond because it will override the absentee parent. I'm all my child has. Yes, it is ideal to have both parents; however, life, as well as the choices we make, lead us elsewhere.

Stop and collect your thoughts. Change your mindset, because all of what you feel and say will spill over onto your child, so fix your leaks. If not, the child will be burdensome to you, taking all that you have to give and present, yet still with a sense of defeat riding them on the inside. They have sucked the life from you, the parent, because you're over-compensating for the absentee. The child caught on early, playing their position, playing it up.

So, you say, "Jane has been cutting school because her father is not in her life." "Johnny has been disrespectful because it's just me, and I have no help." This is because everything you're giving them is not taking the place of the one who is missing in action.

Don't allow your child to become crippled to their environment. You must be positive, speak positively, teaching them how to become resilient to whatever the circumstance of life. It is in their young years that we have the ability to guide their perception of life. So, put your foot down early on. They must be accountable to the discipline and love presented to them, with consistency, from the start. This is how we break the cycle of history repeating itself in and through them — we teach them to do better than what we've done.

CO-PARENTING

You're separately housed... I should only hope that you guys are not competing for the "good guy" title. You all are in a tug-of-war with the child as the rope. Come on, just quit. It takes one of you to throw in the towel. Be the adult that will say, 'I want no part in this.'

Jane learned the intent of both of you and is forced to have two faces — one for each home. She becomes what each home requires her to be. There's no honor in the fact that she doesn't get to show the same face to both parents. Her personality and character are altered due to instability. Instability causes unpredictable behavior as well as erratic changes in mood. If it doesn't destroy the child, in some cases, the child can become the destroyer.

In other words, Jane is in the middle of a mess, struggling to adapt or ready to crumble. She will continuously play and defeat both of you. Jane might say something to one parent, with the truth being altered. Jane knows she is automatically belie-ved because you're so busy building a case against the other parent that you failed to investigate. So, you play superhero against the other parent and have downgraded your integrity for nonsense. Jane takes full advantage and receives no correction; even if one parent gets up the nerve to bring correc-tion, the opponent is at a rise, waiting to spitefully contradict the other.

Stop competing for the spotlight in the child's rearing. Take the focus off yourselves and place it on the well-being of the child. Always stand, not for an appearance, but for what it really is.

Stop competing for the spotlight
in the child's rearing.

The actuality of parenting a child exceeds the appearance of parenting a child. Choose not to be the "good guy," battling for approval and brownie points; be the efficient parent that stands for what's right and, in return, gains the love and respect of your child.

DYSFUNCTIONAL MARRIAGE/ RELATIONSHIP

Children don't get to decide who will be their parents. When they are born into an unhealthy environment, it is not their fault. Your relationship is toxic. You're so engrossed in it, overwhelmed by it, and driven through it that your child's well-being is at stake.

You have disregarded the importance of the child's existence. The provision of love and discipline is not in view. Even other issues such as hygiene, meals, homework, parent-teacher conferences, etc., are unaddressed. Johnny feels unwanted. He internalizes the lack of attention, develops a craving for it, and begins to act out, finding mischief to get into. He hangs out with the wrong crowd for acceptance. Jane is looking for love from all the wrong guys and is taken advantage of due to a lack of attention and love.

A child's well-being is a priority over whomever you can't seem to part with. Children can feel when they are not securely loved or wanted. It's a form of selfishness for an adult to sacrifice the welfare of a child; therefore, do not hesitate to seek help, whether from a friend, family member, or a counselor. Depending on the level of dysfunction, you may even have to run to save your child from a toxic environment.

> **It's a form of selfishness for an adult to sacrifice the welfare of a child.**

Whether you live in the lap of luxury or a humble abode, dysfunction exists in all walks of life. Don't be controlled by the lavishness of things that are obtained by you or whomever you're with. There is no price tag high enough to sacrifice the welfare of children. The substance of a child's character can easily be tainted and screwed up into thinking that, without grand living, there's no inherent worth within themselves.

Decency, cleanliness, structure, and necessities are what's important. Don't be easily impressed while watching others who seem to be doing better than you. Joining the "rat race" will distract you from your parental focus. The high life never guarantees peace. It's an illusion that can look good now, but brings shame later.

In the end, whatever your fortune *or* misfortune regarding family dynamics, be mindful of the role you play in maintaining a healthy balance in relationships, while implementing wisdom to support the well-being of the young people you have been given the awesome responsibility of parenting.

REFLECTION

Describe the parental dynamics in your child or children's life (two-parent home, single-parent home, blended family, etc.). What can you do to ensure that the three parenting keys are being consistently applied?

_____

_____

_____

_____

_____

_____

_____

_____

_____

_____

_____

_____

_____

_____

5

Special
Considerations

Knowing the nature of your child is vital in their rearing. Developing the skills necessary in dealing with each child is based on their personality and development. Do not overlook what they manifest to you. Living in denial and deception will waste time on what could have been accomplished through early alterations and adjustments.

In this chapter, we will discuss the special considerations needed when dealing with children with special needs, the well-mannered child, and the troubled child.

RAISING A CHILD WITH SPECIAL NEEDS

Special needs children are just what they are, and that's "special." They serve a divine purpose in the world. Their deficiency increases our efficiency to become people of quality. How so? They teach us compassion, empathy, patience, and humility. In simplicity, they bring the loss of a heart of substance back to humanity. They bring families closer together, not just physically, but spiritually. They are of significant value. They, too, require love, balance, and even discipline in some instances. Depending on the child's level of need, they also can be balanced to some degree. It may take smaller steps at a slower pace, but it can be done. You, the parent, should be able to watch and recognize what they are capable of learning and at what pace.

Children with special needs can be very bright and intelligent in their own way. They also, at times, can be a bit manipulative with rights, using the disability as a crutch, if allowed. You want to handle them with caution and compassion, with empathy but without pity. Empathy means having the ability to understand and share the feelings of another. Pity brings sorrow and distress alongside empathy. Empathy does well by itself. It drives you to give the help that's needed with a clear and healthy mindset, making it hard for depression to settle in.

Just think, if we all dwelled on our situations, having a comfortable pity seat, life would go on without us, leaving us behind. Fight rather than pity. Your pity will only stifle their ability to grow and see beyond the challenges. Keep in mind that they need balance and structure, as well, to reach their full potential. Pity will only enable them to create the feeling of being useless with no value. They need a sense of normalcy, so don't be shy to set boundaries and use the word "no" when necessary.

Don't deny them or yourself of the proper resources that will help you both to flourish. Therapists, special programs, learning aids, tutoring... addressing your child's different needs; giving various outlets for expression can help with their coping skills while bringing more peace into your home.

We embrace our children's differences with the understanding that it can be of help to other parents in similar situations. Don't tend to the disabled child, tend to the child that happens to be disabled. That means, don't put more emphasis on the disability over the child because the child will feel overlooked or only validated through it.

And don't forget to take care of you. Raising a child with special needs can be physically, mentally, and emotionally exhausting. You are also more likely than other parents to experience anxiety, depression, and other mental health conditions.

THE WELL-MANNERED CHILD

Another critical part of raising your child is teaching them good manners. Knowing, when you're not around, that they can be polite, respectful, and behave themselves benefits everyone. You can have play dates, have public family outings that don't embarrass you and endanger your child.

Good manners — What's that? What does that consist of? Well, as quiet as it's kept, this term goes a long way. If you, the parent, knows what this is, you need to pass it on to your child. For those of you that don't know, let me explain. Do these words ring a bell? Please, may I please, thank you, yes thank you, no thank you, excuse me, I'm sorry, good morning, good evening, good night, have a nice day; it sounds minor; however, it is a big deal. These terms are evidence of good manners.

Here's another word you don't hear anymore... polite! Where has politeness been hiding these days? Is it the pre-K teacher's job to introduce it? Should it now be a curriculum in school? Before they can talk, they should already be introduced and familiarized with these terms. When they begin talking, it should be recited after you. "Tell the nice lady, thank you, Jane."

When you are talking, and your child is old enough to understand, don't allow them to butt in rudely. Tell your child to say "excuse me" before interrupting. If you allow Johnny to do gross things at home, such as talking loudly with a mouth full of food ejecting from it, he will embarrass you outside of the house, just in time for the acquaintances you want to impress to see. Now you're too ashamed to correct him in front of others, but you do it anyway because you know everyone's waiting for you to do so, or maybe it doesn't affect you; that right there is a further problem. You feel there's nothing wrong with it. It's called bad manners.

When Jane wants to be at her friend's house every day, and her friend's mother says it's ok all of the time, teach Jane not to wear out her welcome. You're invited to a barbecue at your boss' house. You arrive with Jane, and Jane, who is old enough to know better, addresses no one. Everyone must speak to her first. This is bad manners. A random person holds the door open for Johnny as he's coming in behind them, and Johnny never says, "thank you."

Bad manners.

....

The world only owes you what you invest in it!

....

Gratitude must be exemplified and implemented to eliminate entitlement. Appreciation of what anyone does for you, no matter how great or small, is noble. It's a beautiful thing when others besides you get to enjoy your child. You're setting them up for success when good manners are taught. You do, they do. You want to be proud when the apple falls close to your tree.

THE TROUBLED CHILD

As an owner of a salon, I had to make sure it ran smoothly so that clients will have professional and peaceful experiences. They would say how my salon was an outlet, a place to unwind, and clear their mind from whatever issues that cluttered it during the day or week. They always felt better inside as well as outside after their visit. However, now and then, we would encounter that mother with the unruly child that wanted to take over every establishment they entered and disrupt everyone's peaceful encounter.

One day, I'm was working on a client, and behind me was another client being serviced. The child she brought with her was running back and forth, so I gave a subtle look to the employee servicing the child's parent. The employee said, "Please have him sit down." The parent told the child to have a seat, and the child started rolling and racing his cars up and down the floor. Now we were walking to-and-fro into a racetrack. How dangerous.

I gave a look to the employee, and she told the child directly, "Please have a seat." The child took a seat and began playing with the equipment that I knew his parents were not prepared to pay for. So, the employee said once again, "Have a seat, please."

By this time, the parent was embarrassed and told the child to come over. The child went to her. After she gently asked him to sit down, he lifted his leg to kick her. As I'm watching this out of the corner of my eye, I began to feel a strange heat escape the top of my head.

In the waiting area, there was a weighted, oversized mirror that hung from the wall above the chairs; the child climbed up on top of the chair and used the frame of the mirror as a racetrack for his car. I said in a monotone voice, "Don't do that." The child looked at me as if I had no right to speak to him. Now, he was going to ignore me by playing more aggressively. The mirror started to move, and in an aggressive tone, I said, "DO NOT PLAY WITH THE MIRROR!" Behind me, in a little small voice, I heard, "He is not yours to yell at..."

Immediately, I stopped what I was doing. I went from reprimanding the child to reprimanding the parent. She told me that he does not respond to yelling. It was clear that he didn't respond to her, or anyone, because he was in full control. He understood that no one was holding him accountable for his disobedience at home, and he had full reign to do as he pleased, but it wasn't going to be under my watch.

The child's safety, along with everyone else's, was compromised. One word, LAWSUIT... for lack of discipline. Just give thought to when you watch the news or social media and see the indignant behavior of people, young and old. Don't become desensitized to the lack of discipline.

> "Tough love may be tough to give, but it is a necessity of life and assurance of positive growth." —T.F. Hodge

We have to work with, travel alongside, be served by, or provide service to those who lack discipline, love, and balance. When you see defiance in your child, nip it in the bud. You are the number one enforcer in their life, so command obedience from their youth. Put your parental "drawers" on, then command and enforce.

REFLECTION

Take a moment to list a couple of behaviors that your child exhibits at home that would not be acceptable to display elsewhere; how will you correct this behavior without infringing on the security they should feel at home? Can you use the three keys effectively in raising a child that has unique concerns?

_____

_____

_____

_____

_____

_____

_____

_____

_____

_____

_____

_____

_____

_____

Final Words
of Wisdom

I was the last of four children, of Caribbean descent, and born in the Bronx, NY. I disliked when my family referred to me as being the baby because, deep inside, I felt I was as mature as my older siblings. I was able to observe my older siblings and learn from a decent amount of their mistakes. I had quite a bit of intel and was somewhat ahead of the game, in regard to the issues of childhood; I even calculated my parents' moves — not to judge, but to learn from them.

My perception was never that of other youth my age. This is why I was sort of a bossy playmate. They didn't observe or take an interest in the things and moments that struck a nerve with me. My motto was: *why go the hard route if you don't have to,* which became the driving force in my grade school years, both academically and socially. If I learned of an easier way with the same results or better, I'm going for it.

Now, over more than a thirty-three-year span, I've had the opportunity to speak with thousands of women, and several men, from all walks of life. My job as an adult is to make people feel, and look, good. So, I will seize any opportunity to help someone avoid traps, dead ends, and needless pain if I possibly can. Knowing that *you can't resolve what you can't comprehend*, I have been able to share bits of straight-to-the-point wisdom on a wide range of topics to those who were open to it, witnessing the lives of many empowered by it.

If this book wasn't written in time for you because your child or children are grown now, speak the truth of your mistakes them, so that they don't make needless mistakes with your grandchildren. If you missed being a wise parent, you could become a wise grandparent. Break the cycle.

Each child matters, and the power we hold in raising our children should never be taken lightly. Based on my journey, I am secure in my faith, knowing that raising children is a sacred task. Not even after getting married did I dream of having children; however, when it happened, I experienced difficulties during both of my pregnancies — nearly dying with the second.

Nevertheless, as challenging as it was, I knew that it was temporary and that the next phase of raising my children was the real challenge. So, I asked God to give me the wisdom to raise them, and He did.

My son and daughter are now twenty-six and twenty-four years old, respectively. I not only love my children; I actually like them. Even more so, it turns out that I truly admire them. Prayerfully, you will be able to say the same.

Until then, come on people... *let's parent!*